THE TWO
DIVINE PROMISES

"The greatest outpouring of God's mercy is reserved for mankind in the twentieth century."

—Fr. Roman Hoppe

A modern version of the famous picture of the Sacred Heart of Jesus posed for by Our Lord Himself during His apparitions to the Polish nun, Sr. Faustina Kowalska (1905-1938). She coached the professional artist who painted the picture, for he could not himself see Our Lord. The original is actually full-length and has powerful promises attached to it.

THE TWO DIVINE PROMISES

by

Fr. Roman Hoppe

SEVENTH EDITION

"I desire the world to be saved, that peace and harmony prevail. It is My wish to reign in the world. I will reign as a result of a better understanding of My Goodness, Love and Mercy, and reparation offered by My chosen soul."

—Words of Our Lord to Sister Josefa

TAN BOOKS AND PUBLISHERS, INC.
Rockford, Illinois 61105

Published with Ecclesiastical Approbation.

Copyright © 1987 by Father Roman Hoppe.

Originally published in 1954 in Polish. First published in English by San Miguel Publishing Co., Detroit, Michigan.

Retypeset by TAN Books and Publishers, Inc. 1987.

Library of Congress Catalog Card Number: 83-50588

ISBN: 0-89555-219-1

Printed and bound in the United States of America.

TAN BOOKS AND PUBLISHERS, INC.
P.O. Box 424
Rockford, Illinois 61105

1987

By faithfully completing this novena of *The Two Divine Promises* we gain abundantly in...

— Faith, hope and charity,

— Union with God,

— The true spirit of ecumenism,

— The spirit of internal peace,

— The love of God and of neighbor,

— The living of the Gospel of Christ in our daily lives and

— The attainment of the grace of salvation for ourselves and for others.

STATEMENT

In accordance with the decrees of Pope Urban VIII, the author states that the alleged graces and occurrences referred to in this booklet have not yet been affirmed by the Church; that the said allegations are to be regarded strictly as personal and private statements; and, in making references to the alleged unusual graces and happenings the author does not wish, in any way, to preclude the subsequent decrees of Holy Mother Church, to whom he remains completely subservient in all matters.

Fr. Roman Hoppe

CONTENTS

Many persons in the following countries of the world are performing this beautiful devotion of *The Two Divine Promises* with great trust and devotion:

Canada

Great Britain

Italy

Poland

Germany

United States

France

Portugal

Czechoslovakia

Spain

New Zealand

The Continent of
South America

PUBLISHER'S PREFACE

The Two Divine Promises are a *private* revelation. Are we duty-bound by Faith to believe in them? Of course not! But are they true? There is no certain way to tell—other than to practice this devotion and wait till we get to Heaven to see for sure. But may we presume that they are true? I would say yes, that we can perform this devotion with relative confidence, having always a conditional attitude in mind and by addressing Our Lord in something of the following manner: "Dear Lord, if *The Two Divine Promises* are in fact true and if Thou wilt indeed reward the faithful execution of this devotion with such glorious results, I hereby offer it to Thee for the purposes Thou hast ordained."

Can we be hurt spiritually by making this devotion? It is difficult to see how, for we are merely employing the Holy Sacrifice of the Mass, the Blessed Eucharist and a few extra prayers—the normal means Our Lord has established for the welfare of our souls and our eternal salvation. May we propagate this devotion? And should we? Of course! What possible harm can be done by promoting attendance at Mass, the Sacraments and prayer? Should we foist upon others our strong conviction that this revelation is true? No, for others may get the wrong idea—for example, that we think a person *has* to believe in *The Two*

Divine Promises, or that we have become "misguided" by placing too much confidence in a private revelation. May we proceed to the practice and promotion of this devotion with a relative moral certitude that it is true? Of course—so long as we always realize that it came from a private source and there is no absolute way to confirm it—and also so long as we submit our minds and our hearts in advance to whatever decision might come from Holy Mother Church in its regard, just as the author has already done in the beginning of this book, by submitting himself in advance to the decisions of the Church, in keeping with the famous decrees of Pope Urban VIII to that effect. For, again, we are practicing and promoting in this devotion nothing more than what Holy Mother the Church asks of us—Mass, Sacraments, prayer, and the urging of these for others as well.

The important question here is whether God has in fact bound Himself to grant the *results* which this devotion claims for itself. Again, we cannot know for sure. We must simply leave that to Him in His great mercy and wait until eternity to find out.

But surely such a powerful sacrificial work as *The Two Divine Promises* call for by us—on behalf of ourselves and others—can only do great, great good toward those ends for which we offer this devotion.

Now, on the other hand, if indeed this devotion

is true, then all the magnificent things Fr. Hoppe says about it are absolutely correct and proper! In fact, he could probably go even further in his acclamation for this devotion.

Finally, in the interest of reinforcing what Fr. Hoppe says in this little booklet about the greatness and power of *The Two Divine Promises*, we have added to the end of this booklet a short appendix which quotes that part of Chapter 6 of St. John's Gospel where Our Blessed Lord speaks about the importance of receiving His Body and Blood and where He gives His mighty promises to those who do. In a very real sense, it would appear that *The Two Divine Promises* devotion is nothing more than an extension of the incredible promises Our Divine Lord Himself has made about the power of receiving His Body and Blood.

The reader, once having finished this book, should then prayerfully meditate upon these words of Our Divine Saviour as quoted in the Appendix and contemplate in silence the meaning of His sweeping claims in *John* 6. Thereafter, the reader should reconsider *The Two Divine Promises* and should ask himself whether indeed—in keeping with the intent of Our Lord's words in Scripture, which words we *can* in fact accept with absolute certainty—*The Two Divine Promises* are not merely an extension of the great promises He makes there. It seems to me that they *are* an extension of His Scriptural promises and that we *can* safely perform this devotion with a high degree of confidence in their truth.

It is for these reasons therefore that we offer readers this new edition of *The Two Divine Promises*, asking that they keep all these preliminary thoughts in mind, and we pray that this devotion will captivate the hearts of many people and will help them grow in the knowledge and love of God by increasing the number of times they assist at Mass and by causing them more frequently to receive the Sacraments, and also that this devotion will thereby bring about an abundant flowing of divine grace into the souls of the poor, misguided people of our reprobate 20th century.

Thomas A. Nelson
Publisher
October 17, 1987

THE MESSAGE OF MERCY
— Given for the 2nd of August, 1979 —

The cataclysm and ensuing punishment for humanity's sins has already been twice deferred by the Divine Mercy through the intercession of the Mother of God, due to the offerings of prayers and practicing of the 90-day novena, *The Two Divine Promises*.

The accumulation of humanity's monstrous sins has diluted the strength of Holy Church's prayers and has made impossible any further deferring of humanity's chastening punishment.

Our most Merciful God and Father has given us an opportunity to reduce humanity's punishment and suffering by shortening *The Two Divine Promises* novena.

As of today, i.e., the *2nd of August, 1979*, *The Two Divine Promises* novena will last thirty days and should encourage all the faithful, religious and priests to undertake the task of obtaining the graces connected with the completion of this novena.

Let us accept this gift, *The Two Divine Promises*, with humility, trust and joy.

Do not delay. Do not wait until God's justice

meets you. Reach out to the source of grace, the Most Merciful Heart of God. Let us offer this novena to Mary, the Mediatrix of God's Graces, and our Mother will favor her children according to the Will of God.

———

Celebrating the Silver Anniversary of this Devotion—25 Years: 1954-1979.

INTRODUCTION

"I desire to save the world through My poorest and most miserable of creatures. I have revealed the great desire of My Heart to you, for through you many souls will come to know My Mercy and Love."
—Words of Our Lord to Sister Benigna

Contemplating the history of mankind and its relation to God, we are confronted with the overwhelming and undisputed fact that the Sovereign God is constantly manifesting to humanity...

—His Goodness
—His Love
—His Unfathomable and Inscrutable Mercy

As often as man falls into sin or grows cold in his relationship with his Creator, the all-loving God continues to display His mercy. His only desire is to bestow eternal life on His creatures, otherwise lost through sin.

Both the Old and the New Testament, as well as the numerous apparitions in the twentieth century, confirm this fact.

In addition to the revelations made by our Immaculate Mother at Fatima in 1917, it is interesting to note that in this present twentieth century

there were *four other successive apparitions,*
namely to...

Sister Benigna (1885-1916), Italy
   The Reminder of God's Mercy
Sister Josefa (1890-1923), France
   The Depth of God's Mercy
Sister Faustina (1905-1938), Poland
   The Trust In God's Mercy
The Two Divine Promises (1954), Poland
   The Realization of God's Mercy

Mankind is steeped in sin, moral decline and
decay in the present age of technological develop-
ment. In this age of atomic and cosmic achieve-
ment, God has been placed in the background.
Truly worthy of our admiration are the enormous
scientific advances of our age, beginning with
atomic energy and ending with planetary space
flights. Alas, such achievements are not sufficient
for mankind! The greater part of the human race
completely disregards Him who holds in His all-
powerful hands, the destiny of the very stars, the
sun, the moon and the planets—many of which
are not even visible to the human eye. Unfor-
tunately, man has forgotten that the primary purpose of his existence in this transient life should
be—first and foremost—*eternal salvation!*

Thus, in a period extremely dangerous to His
creation, He who is love itself again comes to ex-
tend to us His assistance. In a brief interval of time,
four successive apparitions have taken place. So

4

great is the incomprehensible Mercy of God that it is difficult for the human mind to understand how much God desires the salvation of souls in order to endow them with *everlasting happiness*.

In one of His revelations to St. Margaret Mary Alacoque (1647-1690), Our Divine Lord concluded with the following words, "...the end of the world is slowly approaching," while to Sister Faustina (1938), He said, "...for the dreadful day of My Justice is imminent." Can it be that God has made His ultimate revelations in this our twentieth century?

Out of gratitude for God's infinite love toward us, let us prepare *everlasting salvation* for ourselves and for our fellowmen according to the guidelines given us by God Himself. May we ponder and meditate on His words so that they may open our eyes to the wonders that God's Mercy has prepared for us from the creation of the world—*an everlasting inheritance in the kingdom of our Heavenly Father*.

We, therefore, urge all people of good will to undertake the devotion of *The Two Divine Promises* with confidence in God's Mercy, that through this devotion they may bring about...

—A renewal of the face of the earth.
—A long-awaited peace of God on earth.
—A union and peace with God in human souls.

5

Chapter 1

—SISTER BENIGNA—
THE REMINDER OF GOD'S MERCY

*"I desire to regenerate society, but I wish
this regeneration to become a work of love.
I shall use you as an instrument through
whom I shall speak to My creatures and
make known to them My will."*
—Words of Our Lord to Sister Benigna

Sister Maria Benigna Consolata Ferrero was
born in Turin, Italy on August 6, 1885. At the age
of 22, she entered the Congregation of Visitation
nuns in Como, Italy, where she very soon achieved
an intimate union with Christ. She was favored
by God with great spiritual gifts; to make known
to the world the Love and Mercy of God was her
particular vocation. In response to a divine re-
quest, she offered herself as a sacrificial victim (or
victim soul) to obtain peace for the world. After
a short but fruitful life, her Divine Bridegroom
called her to His eternal home on October 1, 1916.
Because of her unwavering faith and love for the
Sacred Heart, Christ chose her as His "little secretary" and repeatedly urged her to *remind* the
world of His Mercy and Love.

The following are some excerpts from Our Lord's
conversations with Sister Maria Benigna Consolata:

"I use My creatures to accomplish My work of Mercy. I Myself select the souls through whom I shall restore the Christian spirit in the world. Such souls have existed in the past, and I will continue to raise similar souls in the future."

"Write, Benigna, Apostle of My Mercy, write that above all I desire to make known that I am full of love, and he who doubts My Goodness inflicts on My Heart untold sorrow."

"Ah, Benigna, if only people would understand how much I love them, how My Heart rejoices when a soul believes in My Love. Alas, very few do believe! Very few, very few! People are not aware what an injustice they cause God when they doubt His Goodness."

"My Love is so little known! If people had a choice to make, they would be inclined to choose a temporal, worldly possession—rather than God Himself."

"O My Beloved, be an Apostle of My Love! Speak for all the world to hear, that I hunger and thirst for souls to receive Me—and this is of so little concern to them."

"God loves mankind so very much; and because they are immortal and will exist eternally, He does everything possible to redeem their souls."

"If a bride saw her beloved hungry and in dire

need, she would, if necessary, even beg alms for him. Seek souls who would receive Me in Holy Communion."

"My compassionate and loving Heart is inflamed with an intense longing for the salvation of souls. When they turn to Me, I can hardly restrain My joy, and I rush forth to meet them."

"Benigna, you are my 'little secretary.' It is your task to write; others will publish your words."

"Write for the glory of My Sacred Heart! The more renowned an artist, the more simple are the tools he uses in order to perfect his masterpiece."

"Behold, it is My wish that you would offer yourself in a specific manner to My Divine Heart for the salvation of sinners. If you further couple your prayers with good deeds, you shall receive so much the easier that which we both so eagerly desire, that is the salvation of souls."
—Words of Our Lord to Sister Benigna

Chapter 2

—SISTER JOSEFA—
THE DEPTH OF GOD'S MERCY

*"I desire the entire world to know that
I am a God of Love, Goodness and Mercy."*
—Words of Our Lord to Sister Josefa

Sister Josefa Maria Menendez was born on April 4, 1890, in Madrid, Spain. After the responsibilities of her early adult years were over, she was received into the Society of the Sacred Heart at Les Feuillants, France. She applied the spirit of the Gospels to her everyday life to such an extent that on the day of her perpetual vows Our Lord privileged her with the grace of the most intimate union with His Heart. She lived only to fulfill His will! After a life filled with great suffering, which she willingly accepted, she died on December 29, 1923. Through her writings, she has given the world an insight into *the depths* of the Mercy and Infinite Goodness of God.

The following quotations taken from her writings reveal God's great Love for souls—a Love unequalled in the history of mankind:

"The world does not know My Merciful Heart. I desire to make It known through you."

"I long to have the whole world read of My ardent desire to forgive and reinstate souls in grace."

"Ah, if only My Heart were understood. People do not know Its Goodness and Mercy. This is My greatest sorrow."

"My Heart finds joy in forgiveness. I have no greater desire nor happiness than to be able to forgive."

"I wish to use you—My insignificant creature—to manifest even more profoundly the Mercy and Love of My Heart. Josefa, the moment one of My creatures falls down on his knees before Me and asks for Mercy, I completely forget his past sins."

"How I long to make known to mankind the Loving Mercy and Forgiveness of My Heart."

"Yes, I yearn to forgive and ask that My chosen souls disclose to the world that My Heart, overflowing with Love and Mercy, awaits sinners."

"How I long to set hearts on fire—the whole world on fire! I invite all of My priests and religious to live a life of complete union with Me."

"I offer you My complete forgiveness. You are Mine, purchased at the price of My own blood. Through you I will save many souls, which were acquired by Me at such a great price. Refuse Me nothing. See how much I love you!"

"See the condescension of My Heart for the love of souls. You too should be inflamed with a burning desire for their salvation."

"My words will have great power over souls and through My grace those who resist Me most will be overcome through love."

"With diabolical craft, Satan contrives numerous ways in which he hopes to spirit away My words, but he will not succeed. My words will continue to bring new life to many souls until the end of time."

—Words of Our Lord to Sister Josefa

Chapter 3

—SISTER FAUSTINA—
THE TRUST IN GOD'S MERCY

"Turning with confidence to the Mercy of God is the greatest gift a soul can offer to his Creator."
—Words of Our Lord to Sister Faustina

Sister Maria Faustina Kowalska was born on August 25, 1905, in Glogowiec, Poland. Even as a teenager she was attracted to the religious life, and her desire was finally realized in 1925, when at the age of 20 she entered the Congregation of the Sisters of Mercy of the Mother of God. The purpose of this community is the care of poor girls who are morally neglected (Magdalens). She made her perpetual vows on March 27, 1937, working before and after very faithfully as a cook and gardener in the various homes of her congregation. As a result of the many extraordinary graces received from Our Lord, she became noted for her deep piety and fullness of spiritual beauty. In the plans of Divine Providence, she was chosen as a "stewardess" of God's Mercy. She was to encourage the entire human race to *trust* in God's incomprehensible and inscrutable Mercy. Following a long illness, she died on October 5, 1938, at the age of 33.

Listed below are a few quotations of Our Lord taken from her writings:

"Write, Secretary of My Mercy, speak of My Great Mercy, for the dreadful day of My Justice is slowly approaching."

"Tell the world about My Mercy and My Love. I am consumed with a desire to pour out My Mercy on human souls. O, how they hurt Me when they refuse My Mercy."

"I cannot punish even the most hardened sinner, if he appeals to My Mercy. He is immediately granted pardon through My incomprehensible and unfathomable Mercy."

"It is My desire that priests should proclaim My Great Mercy toward sinners—who should not fear to approach Me."

"My Daughter, I have disposed My Heart to your wishes; your obligation is to implore Mercy for the entire world."

"No soul will find justification until it turns with confidence to My Mercy."

"Your soul is filled with greater beauty when it meditates on My Passion and Death."

"Tell them, My Daughter, that I am Love and Mercy Itself. When a soul draws near to Me with confidence, My generosity fills it with an abundance of graces far greater than its capacity to contain them—thus overflowing on others."

"Write! Before I come as a Just Judge, I open wide the doors of My Mercy. He who does not wish to avail himself of My Mercy will have to pass through the doors of My Justice."

"As a loving mother shields her infant, so I too will shield, during their entire lives, those who spread devotion to My Mercy. In the hour of their death, I will come, not as a Judge, but as their Merciful Redeemer. In that last hour, a soul has no other defense except My Mercy."

"In the Old Testament, I rebuked My people through My Prophets. Today, I am dispatching you with My Mercy to ailing humanity."

"I have a burning desire to pour out My Mercy on human souls, but they refuse to trust in My Goodness."

"Fight for the salvation of souls. Encourage them to trust in My Mercy."

"Satan has acknowledged to Me that a thousand souls do him less harm than you do when you speak of Almighty God's great Mercy. 'Hardened sinners gain confidence and return to God, while I,' says the devil, 'lose all and by this I am personally persecuted.'"

"If you will meditate on My Passion, you will soon arrive at the state of perfection."

"From Poland will come the spark that will ignite the whole world and prepare it for My final coming."

—Words of Our Lord to Sister Faustina

Chapter 4

—THE TWO DIVINE PROMISES—
THE REALIZATION OF GOD'S MERCY

"Despite My bitter Passion, numerous souls are lost. I am offering mankind the last means of assistance—My Mercy! If they do not take advantage of My Mercy, they will be lost forever."
—Words of Our Lord to Sister Faustina

Our Divine Saviour, through separate revelations to three religious nuns, gives us a practical means to realize the intent of His Divine Promises, the substance of which was handed down to a humble human being selected in Poland by Himself when He spoke to her in these words:

"I have chosen you, and to you I entrust the task of spreading these joyous tidings. The time is approaching when that which the human mind could but slightly conceive will be realized in the most beautiful manner."

"I am He who offered Himself on the Cross of Salvation to My Eternal Father."

"To you I entrust in God's Name a gift of My Father, *The Two Divine Promises*, which will gain for My chosen people a Heavenly Kingdom offered to Me by My Father for those who shall receive it, thanks to My immolation."

"Those who respond to My appeal and attain the grace of eternal salvation for themselves may also—in imitation of My generosity—obtain a similar grace for others."

"I entrust to you those *Two Divine Promises* to pass on to the whole world!"

DIVINE PROMISE

"Each priest who worthily offers the Holy Sacrifice of the Mass for thirty (30) consecutive days and, in addition, makes the Stations of the Cross daily will receive for himself, and another soul selected by him, the assurance of Eternal Salvation."

DIVINE PROMISE

"Likewise, each individual who will receive Holy Communion worthily for thirty (30) consecutive days, and will recite one Our Father and Hail Mary for the welfare of the Holy Catholic Church, will receive for himself and one other soul selected by him, the assurance of Eternal Salvation."

The Two Divine Promises are the confirmation of the Great Divine Plan which God prepared through several selected persons during the span of fifty years of this twentieth century. In this plan God reminds us of His *Infinite Mercy* (Sister Benigna), tells us of its *Depth* (Sister Josefa), implores us to trust in its *Greatness* (Sister Faustina), and in the contents of *The Two Divine Promises* His plan is fully revealed and realized.

The Two Divine Promises contain in themselves the recapitulation of the instructions which Our Lord Jesus Christ entrusted to the three religious nuns. In the contents of the inspired writings of these three nuns, Our Lord very clearly encourages us to a life of penance, which is to be manifested internally and externally in a life filled with sacrifices and founded on love, on obedience to God's call directed to souls, and finally on an ardent desire to save souls, based on continuous prayer.

The Two Divine Promises are an assurance to us that distinct aspects—such as sacrifice, love, God's appeal to souls, eagerness for the salvation of souls, as well as the encouragement to constant prayer, emphasized by Jesus in the writings of the three religious nuns—contain a profound and practical application in the *Two Divine Promises*.

The Two Divine Promises tell us that to comprehend their contents is to begin following the way of sacrifice, which is the awakening in us of love of God and neighbor. Sacrifice and love unite the soul closer to God, cause it to be obedient to His calling, and find their practical application in a zealous appeal for the grace of salvation for oneself and one's neighbor.

The Two Divine Promises encourage us to pursue a life of sacrifice and suffering, for only by such a way of life is it possible to attain the greatest grace of unity with Christ—the Grace of Salvation—and to obtain this grace for others as well.

The Two Divine Promises will, if worthily applied by us, confirm our real love of God and our neighbor.

The Two Divine Promises are God's appeal to mankind to desist from sin and to commence praying for eternal salvation for ourselves and our fellowmen.

The Two Divine Promises are a devotion which should awaken in all Catholics a zeal for the salvation of the souls of mankind. We demonstrate our greatest love towards others, then, when we pray for their salvation.

The Two Divine Promises are the expression of the evangelical spirit of penance—which manifests itself internally in the growth of devotion to the Blessed Eucharist and to Our Lord's Suffering.

The Two Divine Promises are a bonfire of God's Immense Love, emerging from Polish soil, which will set the entire world on fire and prepare the human race for the final coming of Christ.

The Two Divine Promises are a proclamation to all mankind that, out of a nation faithful to Christ for over 1,000 years, whose Patroness and Queen is the Mother of God, comes a concrete plan for the salvation of the world.

The Two Divine Promises are the immemorial expression of God's Will, which He revealed in His

Gospel on the Eucharist: "If any man eat of this bread, he shall live for ever; and the bread that I will give is my flesh, for the life of the world . . . Amen, amen I say unto you: Except you eat the flesh of the Son of man, and drink his blood, you shall not have life in you. He that eateth my flesh, and drinketh my blood, hath everlasting life: and I will raise him up in the last day. For my flesh is meat indeed: and my blood is drink indeed. He that eateth my flesh, and drinketh my blood, abideth in me, and I in him." (*John* 6: 52, 54-57).

Also, on the subject of suffering, where Christ speaks in this manner: "And they that are Christ's, have crucified their flesh, with the vices and concupiscences." (*Gal.* 5:24). "If any man will come after me, let him deny himself, and take up his cross daily, and follow me." (*Lk.* 9:23).

"Christ also suffered for us, leaving you an example that you should follow his steps." (*1 Ptr.* 2:21).

"But God forbid that I should glory, save in the cross of our Lord Jesus Christ; by whom the world is crucified to me, and I to the world." (*Gal.* 6:14).

The Two Divine Promises are the crowning of God's everlasting plan, unfolded and revealed to mankind, directing it to the straight and narrow path which leads to eternal salvation.

The Two Divine Promises are a new and

immense grace, unequalled in the history of the Church. Each person who performs this spiritual exercise, as well as the person for whom this novena is offered, begins to observe more strictly the Commandments of God, the Commandments of the Church, and especially the Commandments of Love. They also learn to inculcate the words of the Gospels into their daily lives.

The Two Divine Promises are the immemorial expression of God's Will, giving all people the equal right to attain the grace of eternal salvation and to bestow this grace upon their fellow creatures.

The Two Divine Promises are an unfailing weapon against sin and evil.

The Two Divine Promises are a devotion which must mobilize all our physical and spiritual energies to undertake an unceasing warfare with Satan, the immemorial foe of our salvation. He will attempt by various and devious means to distract our attention from the goal of eternal salvation.

The Two Divine Promises are a power greater than the atom, which enables the human spirit to soar heavenward to our Heavenly Father with a speed far greater than that of a missile, to a land of everlasting happiness, for all eternity.

The Two Divine Promises are a spiritual exercise

which should encourage priests, religious and laity, in a spirit of love of God and neighbor, to draw down from Almighty God graces that will assure eternal salvation for a countless number of souls.

The Two Divine Promises are the great and effective grace of Divine Mercy which God confers upon each human being for the purpose of a quicker and more lasting unity of our souls with Him. Through the continuous practice of this novena, we are better and more profoundly able to comprehend the actual state of our soul and our relation to God and that our endeavor to unite with Jesus Christ must become the goal of our life upon this earth.

The Two Divine Promises, devoutly performed, shall enhance our comprehension of the words of the Gospel: "How narrow is the gate, and strait is the way that leadeth to life: and few there are that find it!" (*Matt.* 7:14).

Performing this novena under the guidance of divine grace, we are made aware that we must always mortify our senses: our sight, taste, smell, hearing, and touch (which might be called, "the narrow gate"); as well as the three functions of the soul: that is, reason through faith, memory through hope, and will through love of God and our neighbor (these might well be called "the straight way"). Then we shall become more spiritually endowed and we shall understand also that this "Way" is a most difficult one, but the only one, as it is the Gospel Way, directing us to a holy Christian life and to eternal salvation, to which Jesus, again, encourages us in His Gospel: "Be you therefore perfect, as also your heavenly Father is perfect." (*Matt.* 5:48).

The Two Divine Promises are an efficacious novena, particularly for priests, who through their daily offering of the Holy Sacrifice of the Mass and their daily meditations of the Way of the Cross—Christ's Suffering—may introduce into their souls those values of Christ's teachings which He brought upon earth and through which will follow the regeneration of the world and of the souls of mankind. Through the faithful participation in this novena, the clergy may promptly achieve a unity with Jesus Christ—the greatest gift of sanctity—and assist many persons in truly understanding that eternal life is the greatest fortune anyone can possibly attain.

The Two Divine Promises should especially encourage religious nuns to a continued practice of this novena—which for them is a very easy matter—that through their daily union with Jesus Christ in Holy Communion and through praying the Our Father and the Hail Mary for the welfare of the Church they may obtain for themselves the highest grace of sanctity and at the same time assist the Church in its mission of saving souls.

The Two Divine Promises are a novena which, in view of the tasks that the Council imposes on

God's people, shall place an obligation of charity on all Catholics, particularly those in various Catholic organizations and societies, to begin employing this great and efficacious prayer, which will in turn regenerate their personal lives and the social life of the Church. For the greatest love towards our neighbors is manifested when we obtain for them the grace of eternal salvation.

The Two Divine Promises are a great devotion of God's Mercy, which allows us to trust that, should we as the result of our sinful weaknesses, succumb to sin after completing this novena, even then we shall promptly arise from our transgressions and shall begin again to serve God with an even greater love and humility than before.

The Two Divine Promises are the great manifestation of God's Mercy in response to the martyrdom of the millions who lost their lives during the recent holocaustal war. They are a great divine sign indicating the acceptance of the sacrifice made by the innocent multitudes of men, women, children and clergy who remained steadfast in their faith to the very end and deposited in tribute at the throne of the Blessed Trinity, for all of the world to see, their life's blood in witness to Christ.

The Two Divine Promises are a reminder to every Christian, during the 30-day duration of the novena, that the way which leads to the attainment of the grace assuring eternal salvation may often be strewn with sufferings. During this period, we must prepare ourselves to accept various small inconveniences and unpleasantnesses. For the grace of salvation must be earned for oneself and for one's neighbor through the "Cross." All sufferings which may be visited upon us during this period should be united with the sufferings of Our Lord Jesus and offered to the Heavenly Father for the purpose of obtaining the forgiveness of sins and the attainment of this great grace of eternal salvation.

The Two Divine Promises must clearly convince us of the necessity to follow the course of sacrifice and suffering in order to obtain the grace assuring eternal salvation not only for ourselves, but also to obtain this same grace for many others. Sacrifices and sufferings are in essence acts of compensation and atonement for our sins.

Diverse suffering, difficulties and pain, understood in this manner, produce in a soul dedicated to God an element of happiness and satisfaction, and even a desire for suffering, which is a thanksgiving offering garnered for one's Lord and Creator.

During the course of the novena, Christ Our Lord particularly appeals to us to atone for the shortcomings of others through our proffered acts.

The Two Divine Promises are the internal spiritual expression of penance—whose real substance is greater devotion to the Eucharist and the suffering of Jesus Christ—to which Our Lord Jesus Christ continuously encourages us throughout His entire Gospel, as well as of which Our Blessed Mother reminds us most vividly in her revelations during the nineteenth and twentieth centuries at . . .

Paris, France (Miraculous Medal)—1830
LaSalette, France—1846
Lourdes, France—1858
Pontmain, France—1871
Fatima, Portugal—1917
Beauraing, Belgium—1932-1933
Banneux, Belgium—1933
Etc.

Through these great revelations, especially through the encouragement to a profound practice of penance in our Christian lives, Our Blessed Mother prepares us to understand and to receive the greatest gift of God's Mercy, which is the grace of *The Two Divine Promises*.

The Two Divine Promises are a novena which impels all Catholics of good will, in a spirit of ecumenism based upon a pure and supernatural love of God and neighbor, to employ their spiritual and physical powers to win the grace of eternal salvation for our distant and separated brothers, as well as for those near and dear to us.

The Two Divine Promises manifest the vital

power of the Church, enriching itself internally and externally in its journey toward its preordained eternal goal.

The Two Divine Promises is a devotion which, in the plans of Divine Providence, shall by its special power of Sacramental prayer stabilize the Church so that the Barque of Peter, whipped by diverse storms in difficult times, may peacefully sail to its destined goal.

The Two Divine Promises are the foundation stone on which a new era in the history of the Church has been introduced to mankind—an era of spiritual and moral regeneration in the world, an era of intense battle with Satan, the Church's archenemy.

The Two Divine Promises will stay God's wrath, which is impending over mankind and which is brought on by man's ever-increasing degree of sinfulness. They will bring spiritual peace to souls—God's peace on earth—and will prepare mankind for its ultimate meeting with Christ.

The Two Divine Promises are a new and effective form of prayer when offered for people who are responsible for peace in the world and they will obtain from the Good Lord the grace of a true and lasting peace for the entire world.

The Two Divine Promises are an inestimable gift from Almighty God, for which every knee should bend in deep adoration and every human heart burst forth in thanksgiving. This gift of God's Love and Mercy is so great that it exceeds the limits of the human intellect to perceive it.

Here, indeed, is a way of life for those who yearn for eternity.

Chapter 5

RECOMMENDATIONS AND THOUGHTS FOR THOSE UNDERTAKING THE DEVOTION OF *THE TWO DIVINE PROMISES*

"If you will give Me souls, I will give you My Heart. Tell Me, which of us gives more?"
—Words of Our Lord to Sister Josefa

1. Private prayers in accordance with the instructions of *The Two Divine Promises* may be made, just as with the revelations at Lourdes and at Fatima, where the faithful performed those devotions in private for a period of four and thirteen years respectively until the Church publicly sanctioned them.

2. An interrupted novena should be commenced anew.

3. The Divine Lord should be received in the most worthy manner possible, and always in the State of Grace.

4. Before Holy Communion, ask Jesus, "Lord, cleanse my soul of all wickedness that it may be worthy of Thy Grace. Lord, bathe me in Thy Divine Blood."

5. Make known your intention explicitly, by saying, for example, "Lord God, I beg of Thee to grant me in accordance with *The Two Divine Promises* the grace of salvation for my soul, as well as for the soul for whom I pray." (Then mention the person's name.)

6. Despite the fact that we have a free choice of the second person for whose salvation we may pray, it is best to concede this free choice to God, saying something like, "Dear Lord, I will pray, and leave the choice of the second person's soul entirely up to Thee. Please grant us both the grace for which I implore Thee."

7. This devotion may be repeated again and again, indefinitely, during the span of one's lifetime.

8. Upon the completion of the initial novena for oneself and another person, one may and even should, in the spirit of charity and concern for the salvation of others, repeat this novena ever after.

9. After each subsequent novena, the person performing it further enriches and confirms himself in the State of Grace and also obtains this saving grace for still another person.

10. This novena teaches us true love of our neighbor. For the greatest love of one's neighbor is

truly manifested when we help to obtain for him the grace of salvation.

11. During the course of one year, it is possible to obtain this salutary grace for 12 other persons, while at the same time fortifying and increasing our own life of grace.

12. By what other act of good will may we better cooperate with God—except through the utmost concern and exerted effort for our salvation and that of our neighbor?

13. Persons praying this novena should unite their sufferings—which they may encounter during this time—with the sufferings of Jesus and offer them to God the Father for the grace of salvation.

14. During the course of this novena, Satan, the eternal foe of our salvation, will by many means attempt to dissuade us from this devotion for the intention of our salvation; he will attempt to weaken our will and to induce anxiety, so as even temporarily to restrain us in our effort or to cause us doubt. Most often he will suggest the thought that the Church has not yet publicly approved this devotion. He will particularly provoke us to anger and ill will toward our neighbors. In such trying moments, it will take sheer willpower to say to him, "Begone Satan!" Ask Jesus for the strength of endurance.

15. Why does the novena last 30 days? People live in time, and hence it is that in time we ask for graces. For example, the novena of 9 first Fridays lasts 9 months; the novena of 5 first Saturdays lasts for 5 months. This new novena lasts for only one month.

16. Contemplating the meaning of the words dealing with the might of God's Mercy as expressed in *The Two Divine Promises*, one can see that it is a new form of devotion, given to us by Our Lord to enable us to ask through that prayer for the graces necessary for salvation.

17. It is possible that many people of good will, upon learning about this new form of devotion expressed in *The Two Divine Promises*, will have doubts regarding it. It is a proven fact that new devotions, till they are finally proclaimed and approved by the Church, meet with various degrees of acceptance among the people.

18. A great help for all those who seek an understanding of the enormous grace of God's Mercy as set forth in *The Two Divine Promises* would be to acquaint himself with the works by the three saintly nuns, Sister Benigna, Sister Josefa and Sister Faustina, as well as with the revelations of Our Lady at Fatima. Through them, during the first half of the 20th century, Our Lord has prepared mankind for the understanding and acceptance of the greatest grace

of His Mercy, as expressed in *The Two Divine Promises*.

19. Should anyone have doubts about this devotion, there is one very easy piece of advice to offer: Let him but do it just once, and through the blessing of Jesus Christ, the Author of this novena, he will find in his soul the faith he needs to accept the truth of this devotion.

20. A person who will practice this devotion worthily just one time will know with certainty that the Author of *The Two Divine Promises* is the Lord Himself.

Chapter 6

STATEMENTS OF PERSONS ACTIVELY PARTICIPATING IN THE NOVENA OF *THE TWO DIVINE PROMISES*

"I will accomplish My work of Love, through the use of the weak things of this world."
—Words of Our Lord to Sister Faustina.

Nurse, age 60: "I am grateful that I became acquainted with the novena of *The Two Divine Promises,* which I have already begun and which I encourage others to do likewise. I consider myself fortunate to be able to earn this great grace. It has brought me closer to God!"

Nun and Superior of a large Congregation, age 54: "Reflections on the promises emanating from Our Merciful God are a part of my everyday life. I firmly believe that only the love and mercy of God can bring about peace in our souls and in the world."

Widow and Intellectual, age 50: "I am concluding my sixth novena and wish to continue it throughout my life—as long as the Good Lord gives me the necessary strength. Through no merit on my part, but by the grace of the Merciful God,

35

I have truly become a 'new' person."

Nun and Superior, age 45: "My fourth novena is coming to an end. I agree with you, Father, that as we continue this novena, a transformation takes place in each one of us. We begin to see ourselves as we truly are, and our thoughts and desires undergo a change. My love for God is increasing daily. In the past, suffering was something to be avoided, now I welcome it and offer all to Jesus. I am also encouraging my sisters to make this novena."

Prior, age 35: "I pray daily before the miraculous image of Our Lady of Czestochowa, and I trust that through Her intercession the novena of *The Two Divine Promises* will become known to the entire world."

Housewife, age 35: "This is truly a miraculous devotion. It was difficult for me to adjust my schedule to include daily Mass and Communion because of my position, my school-age children and my demanding husband. However, I knew if I made an attempt, the Good Lord would help me. At the conclusion of my novena, my husband, who was an alcoholic and a fallen-away Catholic, fell on his knees before me and vowed he would start a new life. He said he could not explain the change that took place in his soul. The children and I continue to marvel at his transformation. Six months have passed, and my husband is now a model husband, a practicing

Catholic, and has just begun his first novena."

High School Student, age 17: "Since I am naturally slothful, I found it difficult to make this novena. However, I made a total effort and the good Lord helped me to persevere. The results were overwhelming: I resolved to break away from sin, attend the Sacraments frequently and hope to become a priest. I still can't believe it is true!"

Priest and Youth Counselor, age 33: "I noticed a very definite change in the youngsters and teenagers after they began this novena. The little tots who have recently made their First Holy Communion are on fire with love of God, while the older boys who were once very unruly, have become models of perfection. The effects of this novena are tremendous! I have also noticed a change in my own life."

Professor of Mathematics, age 31: "It is an undisputed fact that never in the history of mankind has God been so liberal with His people. When I learned of *The Two Divine Promises*, I was overwhelmed by the great Goodness of Almighty God. I cannot find suitable words to express my sentiments."

Widower, age 48: "I lost all of my possessions in World War II and was on the verge of despair when I became acquainted with the text of *The Two Divine Promises*. For me this represented a ray of hope, and it was! I sincerely trust that in the very near future, the whole world will come to know the immense Mercy of its Creator and that all people everywhere will give thanks for this great gift of God."

Widower, age 64: "The immense Mercy of God manifested to mankind in *The Two Divine Promises* made a very deep impression on me. I am still unable to comprehend the vastness of God's grace. As I continue this novena, I can perceive the many changes that are taking place in me; I see things differently now, and life in general has a deeper meaning for me. I know that God is with me, and my goal in life is Eternity. If more people were acquainted with this devotion, so many more souls would be saved. I trust that in the near future, millions will embrace this novena and thus receive God's choicest grace for themselves and for others."

Artist, age 56: "From the very beginning of this novena, I have experienced a great peace of soul. My everyday trials and tribulations seem of no importance now. My spiritual weakness and unworthiness in receiving Our Lord caused me some distress, but with the help of His grace, this is no longer a source of anxiety for me. I eagerly look forward to that union with my Creator! The Mercy of God is limitless!"

Housewife, age 41: "I would like to see this revelation spread to the four corners of the world, so that everyone could take advantage of it. Only then will the world enjoy true peace of mind and happiness. When this happens, there will be no need for psychiatric care."

Friar and Philosopher, age 43: "There was much talk at the last Council about Ecumenism. *The Two Divine Promises* present an occasion to put Ecumenism into practice."

Monsignor and Doctor of Theology, age 60: "Every priest should often reflect on the method which Our Divine Lord chose to present this opportunity for the grace of salvation. If we truly love our neighbors as ourselves, we will fulfill the first and greatest of all commandments and thus gain the grace of eternal salvation for a countless number of souls. This will confirm our love of God and neighbor."

Public Official, age 60: "I realize that peace on earth depends on mankind. The Good Lord could intervene, but He prefers to act through men. At the present time, there are some 120 nations in the world. If a group of people volunteered to make the novena of *The Two Divine Promises* for the heads of these nations, I am sure they would come to an understanding and there would be peace."

Mother of Large Family, age 68: "I have decided to make the novena of *The Two Divine Promises* for each of my children. God is so good to give us this grace!"

Priest, age 38: "As soon as I learned of this devotion, I decided to begin my first novena. Since then I have made many such novenas during the past few years. At the present time I have but one goal in life: to obtain the grace of eternal salvation for as many souls as I possibly can. Thus, I will not stand empty-handed before my Creator at the Last Judgment!"

Career Officer, age 69: "This novena means for me an inconceivable mercy of God. In this day and age, when through lust and immorality, souls are drawn to the very brink of Hell, this devotion is truly a gift from Heaven. If only the entire world could learn of *The Two Divine Promises*, it would hasten the day when millions of souls would be saved for Christ. Since making this novena, I am filled with a joy that words cannot express. Each day brings a greater union with my Creator and peace of soul that defies comprehension."

Nun, age 37: "I have spent 20 years as a member of an active-contemplative order. I would like to dedicate the remainder of my life to obtain the salvation of hardened and forgotten sinners. I am praying in particular that more and more people will learn of this devotion."

Engineer and Academic Curriculum Coordinator at an Institute of Technology, age 52: "Man must mature spiritually. The human soul must experience a certain technological process transforming its internal structure. The attainment of an inner-awareness of one's final destination is the catalyst in the change which accompanies the self-imposed rigor prescribed in *The Two Divine Promises.*

"When I completed the first segment of the four-score-and-ten-day novena [the novena was originally 90 days], a difficult and tedious task, I came to the realization that here, indeed, God had bestowed upon man a new grace, designed for the present period of his existence, to enable him to achieve his purpose, which is the summit of 'Mount Carmel'—eternal salvation.

"I see no other way to avoid the impending catastrophe 'at the turning point of mankind's history,' except to cooperate in the name of 'the love of one's neighbor,' in saving souls in accordance with the guidelines of *The Two Divine Promises.*"

Bishop, age 49: "Human nature is virtually weak. It therefore needs constant incentives to advance forward.

"An example of this may be observed in the history of the various new devotions which were heavenly inspired to assist mankind throughout different periods of time. The devotion of *The Two Divine Promises* is a revelation—it is something new, so far unencountered in the history of the Church. Profoundly understood, this devotion can lead mankind to the One Fold of Christ.

"Possibly, since the time of His coming upon this earth, Christ's concern for the eternal salvation of the world has not been so apparent as it is today.

"We should all give this our utmost attention...and undertake the challenging aspect of performing this novena, not only for ourselves, but foremost for others, bearing in mind the words of our Lord Jesus that there is greater rejoicing in Heaven over one repentant sinner than 99 others who are just..."

Appendix 1

ST. JOHN'S GOSPEL
CHAPTER 6, VERSES 26-70
(Added to the present edition by the Publishers.)

The reader would do well to read prayerfully and meditatively the powerful words of Our Lord Jesus Christ with regard to receiving the Holy Eucharist, His Body and Blood, as recorded in St. John's Gospel, Chapter 6, Verses 26 to 70.

The entire text is quoted here without break to give the reader the full sense of Our Lord's words. It is important, in this regard, to remember that just the previous day Our Lord had fed the 5,000 in the countryside, multiplying five barley loaves and two fishes. Now the Gospel says, "The men therefore sat down, in number about five thousand." (*Jn.* 6:10). Including women and children in this throng, one could easily imagine there to have been 12,000 to 20,000 people over all.

Because Our Lord knew the people would come to take Him by force and make Him king, He "fled again into the mountain, himself alone." (*Jn.* 6:15). It was on the next day, when the people had caught up with Our Lord, that the following episode transpired. They had just asked Him, "Rabbi, when camest thou hither?" (*Jn.* 6:25).

And "Jesus answered them, and said: Amen, amen I say to you, you seek me, not because you have seen miracles, but because you did eat of the loaves, and were filled. Labour not for the meat which perisheth, but for that which endureth unto life everlasting, which the Son of man will give you. For him hath God, the Father sealed.

"They said therefore unto him: What shall we do, that we may work the works of God?

"Jesus answered, and said to them: This is the work of God, that you believe in him whom he hath sent.

"They said therefore to him: What sign therefore dost thou show, that we may see, and may believe thee? What dost thou work? Our fathers did eat manna in the desert, as it is written: *He gave them bread from heaven to eat.*

"Then Jesus said to them: Amen, amen I say to you; Moses gave you not bread from heaven, but my Father giveth you the true bread from heaven. For the bread of God is that which cometh down from heaven, and giveth life to the world.

"They said therefore unto him: Lord, give us always this bread.

"And Jesus said to them: I am the bread of life: he that cometh to me shall not hunger: and he that believeth in me shall never thirst. But I said unto you, that you also have seen me, and you believe not. All that the Father giveth to me shall come to me; and him that cometh to me, I will not cast out. Because I came down from heaven, not to do my own will, but the will of him that sent me. Now this is the will of the Father who sent me: that of all that he hath given me, I should lose nothing; but should raise it up again in the last day. And this is the will of my Father that sent me: that every one who seeth the Son, and believeth in him, may have life everlasting, and I will raise him in the last day.

"The Jews therefore murmured at him, because he had said: I am the living bread which came down from heaven. And they said: Is not this Jesus, the son of Joseph, whose father and mother we know? How then saith he, I came down from heaven?

"Jesus therefore answered, and said to them: Murmur not among yourselves. No man can come to me, except the Father, who hath sent me, draw him; and I will raise him up in the last day. It is written in the prophets: *And they shall all be taught of God.* Every one that hath heard of the Father, and hath learned, cometh to me. Not that any man hath seen the Father; but he who is of God, he hath seen the Father. Amen, amen I say unto you: He that believeth in me, hath everlasting life.

"I am the bread of life. Your fathers did eat

manna in the desert, and are dead. This is the bread which cometh down from heaven; that if any man eat of it, he may not die. I am the living bread which came down from heaven. If any man eat of this bread, he shall live for ever; and the bread that I will give, is my flesh, for the life of the world.

"The Jews therefore strove among themselves, saying: How can this man give us his flesh to eat?

"Then Jesus said to them: Amen, amen I say unto you: Except you eat the flesh of the Son of man, and drink his blood, you shall not have life in you. He that eateth my flesh, and drinketh my blood, hath everlasting life: and I will raise him up in the last day. For my flesh is meat indeed: and my blood is drink indeed. He that eateth my flesh, and drinketh my blood, abideth in me, and I in him. As the living Father hath sent me, and I live by the Father; so he that eateth me, the same also shall live by me. This is the bread that came down from heaven. Not as your fathers did eat manna, and are dead. He that eateth this bread, shall live for ever.

"These things he said, teaching in the synagogue, in Capharnaum. Many therefore of his disciples, hearing it, said: This saying is hard, and who can hear it?

"But Jesus, knowing in himself, that his disciples murmured at this, said to them: Doth this scandalize you? If then you shall see the Son of man ascend up where he was before? It is the spirit that quickeneth: the flesh profiteth nothing. The words that I have spoken to you, are spirit and life. But there are some of you that believe not. For Jesus knew from the beginning, who they were that did not believe, and who he was, that would betray him. And he said: Therefore did I say to you, that no man can come to me, unless it be given him by my Father.

"After this many of his disciples went back; and walked no more with him. Then Jesus said to the twelve: Will you also go away?

"And Simon Peter answered him: Lord, to whom shall we go? thou hast the words of eternal life. And we have believed and have known, that thou art the Christ, the Son of God."

—*John* 6:26-70

Appendix 2

HOW TO GAIN
A PLENARY INDULGENCE
(Added to this present edition by the Publishers.)

The value of gaining a "plenary indulgence" is that, should one die immediately afterwards, that is, before committing any other sins, he or she would go straight to Heaven and not have to spend any time in Purgatory. However, since there is so much confusion over indulgences in general and because "temporal punishment" is so poorly understood, it is best to consider the entire teaching of the Church on this subject.

The Catholic Church, in view of her "power of the keys," that is of loosing and binding in the area of Church discipline (which binds Catholics morally), and thereby of her right to lay down certain prerequisites for gaining grace in certain circumstances, has the right to grant "indulgences" to certain acts performed according to the norms she specifies.

By definition, an *indulgence* is the remission of *part* or *all* of the *temporal punishment* resulting from the commission of sin. If *part* of the temporal punishment is remitted, the indulgence is called a *partial* indulgence; if *all* of the temporal punishment is remitted, the indulgence is called a *plenary* indulgence.

The key to understanding indulgences is to have a proper understanding of just what *temporal punishment* is. As the name indicates, *temporal* punishment is punishment *in time* or *for a time*; *tempus* in Latin means "time." This temporal punishment is connected to all sin, and remains even after sin has been forgiven; it exists in the form of a "spiritual debt"—the counterpart, so to speak, of the *merit* we gain for our good works. Temporal punishment due to sin—our "spiritual debt"—must be repaid, even though our sins have already been forgiven. For example, if you break a neighbor's window, you might go and ask for forgiveness and in fact obtain it; however, you will still be expected to pay for the neighbor's window. The *debt* of needing to pay for the window in this case corresponds to the *temporal punishment due to sin.*

The way we pay the debt of temporal punishment due to our sins is by *prayer, penance, sacrifice, good works* and *alms giving,* but particularly by *gaining indulgences.* Now indulgences are nothing but a special remission of debt, resulting from prayers, etc., that we perform. In the divine plan, this remission is applied against our *temporal punishment* (or "spiritual debts") until the debts are paid off.

For many prayers and good works the Church grants a *partial* indulgence to those Catholics who perform them with the intention of gaining the attached indulgence. However, to certain specific prayers and spiritual acts, specially designated by the Church, and generally longer and more difficult to perform, the Church attaches a *plenary* indulgence, that is a *full* indulgence, or one that takes away *all* the temporal punishment due for the sins that a person has committed and has had forgiven but that have not yet been "paid for" or "expiated."

To gain a partial indulgence, a Catholic must simply perform the prescribed work in the state of grace—that is, free of having committed a mortal sin that remains unforgiven. *To gain a plenary indulgence,* however, several additional factors must also be present. All together, they are the following:

1. *The person must be in the state of grace,* that is free from mortal sin that has not been confessed and forgiven in the Sacrament of Penance.

2. *The recipient must have been to Confession within several days* of performing the prescribed work. (Several days afterwards also qualifies, but the indulgence is not earned until this requirement is fulfilled.)

3. *The person must receive Holy Communion within several days before or after performing the work* to which the indulgence is attached—but preferably on the same day.

4. *The recipient must perform the prescribed work with the intention of gaining the indulgence.* This "work" can be 1) saying the Rosary—5 decades—with meditation on the respective mysteries in a Catholic church or public oratory, in a family group, in a religious community or in a pious association; 2) making the Stations of the Cross; 3) making a 30-minute visit to the Blessed Sacrament; 4) piously reading Sacred Scripture for one-half hour; or 5) any other of a number of specific "works" designated by the Church in her *Enchiridion of Indulgences.* But one must remember that all the other conditions must also be filled.

5. *The person must say some prayers for the Pope's intentions.* An *Our Father* and a *Hail Mary* will suffice.

6. *The recipient must be free from all attachment to sin.* Even though a person might still sin, as we all do, or even be inclined to an habitual sin, such as using God's name in vain, yet so long as the *attachment* to the sin, or the *desire* to commit it is *absent* from the person's soul, he or she would be considered "free from attachment to sin."

7. *Only one plenary indulgence may be gained per day.*

What is of great consolation to those who have recently lost deceased loved ones is the fact that indulgences can be gained for the Poor Souls in Purgatory. And in the case of a *plenary* indulgence gained for a Poor Soul in Purgatory, that soul, if it pleases God, would be released immediately from Purgatory and would thereby wing his or her way to Heaven. Plus, the general consensus of the saints who have been especially graced with revelations about Purgatory is that plenary indulgences gained for the Poor Souls *are also imputed to the person who gains them.* Thus, it is generally believed, especially from a revelation of St. Gertrude the Great, which she discloses in her *Revelations,* that the person helping the Poor Souls will himself still receive all the benefits of the plenary indulgences he has gained for them.

The *momentous import* of what has been said above may not appear immediately to the reader. What has just been said is this: If you will go to Confession every week, then every time you attend Mass and receive Holy Communion, *you have it within your power to release a soul from Purgatory* (if it pleases God) *simply by remaining after Mass and offering the Holy Rosary before the Blessed Sacrament,* or by saying the Rosary with your family or with your community. (Or, you can perform any one of a number of "works" to which Holy Church has attached a plenary indulgence. See number 4 above.)